EPHRAIM MCCLEARY

Beginners Guide to Investing in the Bonds Market

Copyright © 2024 by Ephraim McCleary

All rights reserved. No part of this publication may be reproduced, stored or transmitted in any form or by any means, electronic, mechanical, photocopying, recording, scanning, or
otherwise without written permission from the publisher. It is illegal to copy this book, post it to a website, or distribute it by any other means without permission.

Ephraim McCleary asserts the moral right to be identified as the author of this work.

Ephraim McCleary has no responsibility for the persistence or accuracy of URLs for external or third-party Internet Websites referred to in this publication and does not guarantee that any content on such Websites is, or will remain, accurate or appropriate.

Designations used by companies to distinguish their products are often claimed as trademarks. All brand names and product names used in this book and on its cover are trade names,
service marks, trademarks and registered trademarks of their respective owners. The publishers and the book are not
associated with any product or vendor mentioned in this book.

None of the companies referenced within the book have endorsed the book.

First edition

This book was professionally typeset on Reedsy. Find out more at reedsy.com

Contents

1 Chapter 1	1
2 Chapter 2	4
3 Chapter 3	7
4 Chapter 4	10
5 Chapter 5	13
6 Chapter 6	16
7 Chapter 7	19
8 Chapter 8	22
9 Chapter 9	25
10 Chapter 10	28

Chapter 1

Chapter 1: The Basics of Bonds

What Are Bonds? Bonds are a form of investment that represents a loan made by an investor to a borrower. Typically, the borrower can be a corporation, a municipality, or a government. The bond issuer commits to paying back the borrowed funds on a predetermined date, known as the maturity date, along with periodic interest payments, referred to as coupons. Bonds are thus considered a fixed-income security due to the regular income stream they provide.

Understanding Bond Terms and Concepts

To navigate the bond market effectively, it's crucial to understand the following key terms and concepts:

- **Par Value**: Also known as the face value, it is the amount that the bond issuer agrees to repay the bondholder at maturity. Par value is usually set at $1,000 for corporate bonds.
- **Coupon Rate**: This is the interest rate that the bond issuer pays on the bond's par value. It is expressed as a percentage and determines the periodic interest payments that the bondholders receive.

- **Maturity**: The maturity date is when the bond's principal amount is due to be paid back to the bondholder. Bonds can have short-term (less than 3 years), medium-term (4-10 years), or long-term (more than 10 years) maturities.
- **Yield**: Yield is a measure of return on a bond investment and is usually expressed as an annual percentage. It takes into account the coupon rate, the price of the bond, and the time remaining until maturity.

Types of Bonds

Bonds come in various types, each catering to different market segments and investment strategies:

- **Government Bonds**: Issued by national governments, these bonds are considered among the safest investments since they are backed by the issuing country's ability to tax its citizens. Examples include U.S. Treasury bonds.
- **Corporate Bonds**: Issued by companies, corporate bonds usually offer higher yields than government bonds due to the higher risk of default. They are rated by credit rating agencies to help investors assess this risk.
- **Municipal Bonds**: Issued by states, cities, or other local government entities, these bonds often provide tax-exempt interest income, making them attractive to investors in higher tax brackets.
- **International Bonds**: Issued by foreign governments or

corporations, these bonds expose investors to international markets and diversify investment portfolios across global economies.

How Bonds Differ from Stocks

While both bonds and stocks are securities, they represent different types of investment and carry distinct characteristics:

- **Ownership vs. Loan**: Stocks represent ownership shares in a company, giving shareholders a claim on the company's assets and earnings. Bonds, on the other hand, represent a loan from the investor to the issuer, with a promise of repayment plus interest.
- **Risk and Return**: Generally, stocks offer higher potential returns than bonds but come with higher volatility and risk. Bonds typically offer lower returns but provide a more stable and predictable income stream.
- **Income vs. Growth**: Bonds are primarily income investments, providing regular interest payments. Stocks are considered growth investments, with returns coming from an increase in stock price or dividends.

This chapter has laid the foundation for understanding the basic principles of bonds, the different types available, and how they contrast with stocks. As we move forward, we will delve deeper into the intricacies of bond investing, including how to assess bond investments and build a bond portfolio tailored to individual financial goals.

Would you like to explore any specific topic in more detail or proceed to the next chapter focusing on more advanced bond investment strategies?

Chapter 2

Chapter 2: Benefits and Risks of Bond Investing

Bond investing offers a unique blend of benefits and risks that can suit a variety of investment strategies and objectives. Understanding these can help investors make informed decisions and tailor their bond investments to align with their risk tolerance and financial goals.

Income Generation through Bonds

One of the primary benefits of investing in bonds is the potential for income generation. Bonds typically pay interest semi-annually, providing bondholders with a steady income stream. This feature makes bonds particularly attractive to investors seeking regular income, such as retirees.

Diversification Benefits

Bonds often exhibit less volatility compared to stocks, making them an excellent tool for portfolio diversification. By allocating assets across different types of investments, investors can reduce the overall risk of their portfolio. During periods of stock market downturns, bonds, especially government and high-quality corporate bonds, tend to perform better, thus offering a cushion against losses.

Interest Rate Risk

Interest rate risk is a critical factor to consider when investing in bonds. When interest rates rise, bond prices typically fall, and vice versa. This inverse relationship means that bondholders face the risk of declining bond prices if interest rates increase. Bonds with longer maturities are usually more sensitive to interest rate changes, making them more volatile in a changing rate environment.

Credit Risk

Credit risk refers to the risk that a bond issuer will default on its obligation to pay interest and return the principal at maturity. Corporate bonds generally carry a higher credit risk compared to government bonds. Credit ratings, provided by agencies such as Moody's, Standard & Poor's, and Fitch, can help investors assess the creditworthiness of bond issuers.

Inflation Risk

Inflation risk, or the risk that inflation will erode the purchasing power of future interest payments and principal, is another important consideration. Inflation can particularly affect longterm bondholders, as the real value of the interest payments received over time may decline.

Assessing and Mitigating Risks

Investors can take several steps to assess and mitigate the risks associated with bond investing:

1. **Diversification**: By spreading investments across various

types of bonds (e.g., government, corporate, municipal) and sectors, investors can reduce the impact of a single bond's performance on their overall portfolio.
2. **Duration Management**: Investing in bonds with different maturities can help manage interest rate risk. Shorter duration bonds are less sensitive to interest rate changes.
3. **Credit Quality**: Focusing on bonds with high credit ratings can mitigate credit risk. However, for higher returns, investors may consider lower-rated bonds with a thorough analysis of the issuer's financial health.
4. **Laddering**: Bond laddering involves purchasing bonds with varying maturities. As each bond matures, the principal is reinvested in a new long-term bond, helping to manage interest rate risk and provide liquidity.
5. **Inflation**-Protected Securities: Investing in inflation protected securities, such as Treasury Inflation-Protected Securities (TIPS), can help shield investors from inflation risk.

This chapter has explored the various benefits and risks associated with bond investing, highlighting the importance of income generation, diversification, and the strategies to mitigate inherent risks like interest rate fluctuations, credit default, and inflation. As investors become more familiar with these concepts, they can better position their portfolios to achieve their desired balance of risk and return.

Ready to delve into strategies for building a successful bond portfolio, or is there a particular aspect you'd like to explore further?

Chapter 3

Chapter 3: Navigating the Bond Market

Understanding and navigating the bond market requires a grasp of how economic indicators, monetary policy, and bond ratings influence bond prices and market trends. This knowledge not only aids in making informed investment decisions but also in anticipating market movements.

Impact of Economic Indicators and Monetary Policy on Bond Prices

Economic indicators and monetary policies play pivotal roles in shaping the bond market landscape. Here's how:

- **Economic Indicators**: Key indicators such as inflation rates, unemployment figures, and GDP growth can significantly affect bond prices. For instance, high inflation usually leads to higher interest rates, which negatively impact bond prices. Conversely, signs of economic slowdown might lead to lower interest rates, boosting bond prices.

- **Monetary Policy**: Central banks' policies on interest rates directly influence bond markets. An interest rate hike typically lowers bond prices, while rate cuts generally lead to higher bond prices. Investors monitor central bank announcements and policy meetings closely to gauge potential market movements.

Following and Interpreting Bond Market Trends

To stay ahead, investors should develop a routine for tracking and interpreting bond market movements:

1. **Market Indices and Benchmarks**: Follow major bond market indices, such as the Bloomberg Barclays Global Aggregate Bond Index, to get a sense of overall market performance.
2. **Yield Curves**: The yield curve, which plots the yields of bonds with different maturities, is a crucial indicator of market sentiment and economic outlook. An inverted yield curve, where short-term yields are higher than longterm yields, often signals economic recession.
3. News and Reports: Economic news, central bank announcements, and financial reports can provide insights into potential market shifts. Staying informed helps investors anticipate changes in bond prices and yields.

Understanding Bond Ratings

Bond ratings are critical for assessing the risk associated with different bonds:

- **Investment Grade**: Bonds rated BBB- or higher by Standard & Poor's or Baa3 or higher by Moody's are considered investment grade. These bonds carry lower credit risk and are preferred by risk-averse investors.
- **High Yield**: Also known as junk bonds, these are rated BB+ or lower by Standard & Poor's or Ba1 or lower by Moody's. High yield bonds offer higher interest rates to compensate for the higher risk of default.

Investors should consider bond ratings alongside their investment goals and risk tolerance. While investment-grade bonds offer stability and lower risk, high-yield bonds can provide substantial income potential at a higher risk.

This chapter delves into the fundamentals of understanding and navigating the bond market, emphasizing the importance of economic indicators, monetary policy, and bond ratings. By mastering these concepts, investors can enhance their ability to make strategic decisions and optimize their bond investments.

Would you like to proceed with strategies for building and managing a bond portfolio, or is there an aspect of the bond market you wish to explore further?

Chapter 4

Chapter 4: Crafting Your Bond Investment Strategy

Developing a coherent bond investment strategy is pivotal for achieving your financial objectives while adhering to your risk tolerance. This chapter guides you through setting investment goals, determining risk tolerance, and formulating a diversified bond portfolio tailored to your income or growth aspirations.

Setting Investment Goals and Risk Tolerance

Begin by articulating clear investment goals and understanding your risk tolerance, as these will dictate your bond investment strategy:

- **Investment Goals**: Identify what you aim to achieve through your bond investments. Goals can range from preserving capital and generating steady income to accumulating wealth over the long term.
- **Risk Tolerance**: Assess your comfort level with investment risk. Consider factors such as investment horizon, financial situation, and your reaction to potential losses. Your risk tolerance will influence the types of bonds you invest in and the portfolio's overall risk profile.

Building a Diversified Bond Portfolio

Diversification is a cornerstone of successful bond investing. A well-diversified bond portfolio can help manage risk and smooth out returns over time. Here's how to build one:

1. **Mix Different Types of Bonds**: Incorporate a variety of bonds—government, corporate, municipal, and international bonds—into your portfolio. Each type of bond carries different risk and return characteristics, contributing to diversification.
2. **Vary Maturities**: Include bonds with different maturities to manage interest rate risk. A laddered portfolio, where bonds mature at staggered intervals, can provide regular income and opportunities to reinvest at higher rates.
3. **Consider Credit Qualities**: Balance your portfolio with a mix of investment-grade and high-yield bonds according to your risk tolerance. While investment-grade bonds offer stability, high-yield bonds can boost portfolio returns.

Strategies for Income Versus Growth

Your investment strategy should align with your preference for income generation, capital growth, or a combination of both:

- **Income Strategy**: If generating regular income is your goal, focus on bonds with higher coupon rates and shorter

to medium maturities. Investment-grade corporate bonds, municipal bonds, and high-yield bonds can be suitable choices.
- **Growth Strategy**: For investors aiming at capital appreciation, consider bonds with the potential for price appreciation. This might involve investing in longerduration bonds or lower-rated bonds with higher yield potential, albeit at a higher risk.
- **Balanced Approach**: A balanced strategy might include a mix of bonds that offer both income and growth potential, tailored to achieve a moderate level of risk while providing steady income.

Crafting a bond investment strategy that aligns with your financial goals and risk tolerance is essential for navigating the complexities of the bond market. Whether you're focused on income generation, capital growth, or a balance of both, a diversified bond portfolio is key to achieving your investment objectives.

As we conclude this chapter, are there specific aspects of bond investment strategies you'd like to delve deeper into, or would you prefer to explore advanced topics such as bond valuation techniques and market analysis methods?

Chapter 5

Chapter 5: Bond Valuation and Yield

Mastering the fundamentals of bond valuation and understanding yield are crucial for any investor looking to make informed decisions in the bond market. This chapter covers the essential calculations for bond prices and yields, explores the significance of the yield curve, and elucidates the relationship between bond prices and interest rates.

How to Calculate Bond Prices and Yields

Bond valuation typically revolves around calculating the present value of all future cash flows expected from the bond (i.e., coupon payments and the return of the principal at maturity). Here's a simplified overview:

- **Bond Prices:** The price of a bond is determined by discounting the bond's future interest payments and its principal repayment at the current market interest rate.

The formula involves calculating the present value of the bond's future cash flows.
- **Yield**: The yield of a bond is a measure of return based on the coupon rate and the current price of the bond. There are several types of yields, including current yield, yield to maturity (YTM), and yield to call (YTC). YTM is the most comprehensive, considering the total returns expected if the bond is held to maturity.

Understanding the Yield Curve and Its Implications

The yield curve is a graphical representation showing the relationship between the yield (interest rate) and the term to maturity of debt for a given borrower in a given currency. Here are its key implications:

- **Economic Indications**: A normal yield curve (upward sloping) suggests economic growth expectations. An inverted yield curve (downward sloping) is often seen as a predictor of economic recession.
- **Investment Strategy**: The shape of the yield curve can influence bond investment decisions. For example, in a steep yield curve environment, long-term bonds may offer significantly higher yields to compensate for the risk of holding them longer.

The Relationship Between Bond Prices and Interest Rates

Understanding the inverse relationship between bond prices and interest rates is fundamental:

- **Interest Rate Increases**: When market interest rates rise, the price of existing bonds falls to adjust the yield upward,
making them competitive with newly issued bonds with higher coupon rates.
- **Interest Rate Decreases**: Conversely, if market interest rates fall, the price of existing bonds rises, as their higher coupon payments are more valuable, increasing the bond's price to adjust the yield downward.

This relationship is vital for investors, as it affects the market value of their bond investments and their portfolio's overall interest rate risk.

Understanding bond valuation and yield, the implications of the yield curve, and the relationship between bond prices and interest rates are essential for navigating the bond market effectively. This knowledge not only aids in making informed investment decisions but also in strategically managing a bond portfolio in varying market conditions.

Would you like to continue with more advanced topics, such as analyzing market trends or risk management techniques, or perhaps review any concepts in more detail?

Chapter 6

Chapter 6: How to Buy and Sell Bonds

Investing in bonds can be accomplished through several avenues, each with its advantages and considerations. This chapter explores the process of purchasing individual bonds, investing in bond funds and ETFs, and leveraging online platforms and direct government purchases.

Purchasing Individual Bonds through Brokers

- **Broker-Dealer Networks**: Individual bonds can be bought and sold through broker-dealers. Investors can choose from government, corporate, or municipal bonds available in the broker's inventory.
- **Considerations**: When purchasing through brokers, it's important to understand the markup or commission that may be applied. Comparing prices and yields

offered by different brokers can ensure you get the best deal.
- Research: Due diligence is crucial when selecting bonds. Investors should consider the bond's rating, yield, maturity, and the issuer's financial stability.

Investing in Bond Funds and ETFs

- **Bond Funds**: These are mutual funds that invest in a diversified portfolio of bonds. Bond funds offer professional management and diversification but come with management fees. Investors buy shares in the fund, and returns are distributed as dividends.
- **ETFs (Exchange-Traded Funds)**: Bond ETFs operate similarly to bond funds but are traded on stock exchanges like individual stocks. They offer liquidity and lower fees compared to mutual funds but fluctuate in price throughout the trading day.
- **Choosing the Right Investment:** Whether to invest in bond funds or ETFs depends on one's investment strategy, need for liquidity, and sensitivity to fees. Both options provide exposure to a broad range of bonds, simplifying diversification.

The Role of Online Platforms and Direct Government Purchases

- **Online Trading Platforms**: The advent of online platforms has simplified the process of buying and selling bonds. These platforms offer access to a wide

array of bonds, real-time pricing, and lower transaction costs compared to traditional brokerage firms.
- **Direct Government Purchases**: Investors can also purchase government bonds directly from the issuing government. For example, in the United States, Treasury securities can be bought through the Treasury Direct website. This method eliminates broker fees and allows investors to buy new issues directly from the government.

This chapter has outlined the primary methods for buying and selling bonds, including through brokers, bond funds, ETFs, online platforms, and direct purchases from governments. Each method has its unique advantages and considerations, from the personalized selection and research required when buying individual bonds to the ease and diversification offered by bond funds and ETFs. The choice of platform—whether online, through a broker, or directly from the government—depends on the investor's strategy, preferences, and the specific types of bonds they are interested in.

Would you like to explore advanced investment strategies, delve into the nuances of analyzing bond markets, or need clarification on any of the topics covered so far?

Chapter 7

Chapter 7: Advanced Bond Investment Strategies

For investors looking to optimize their bond portfolios further, advanced strategies and concepts like bond laddering, duration, convexity, and tax-efficient investing can provide nuanced control over interest rate risks and tax liabilities. This chapter delves into these sophisticated techniques, offering insights into maximizing returns while mitigating risks.

Bond Laddering and Its Benefits

- **Bond Laddering**: This strategy involves purchasing bonds with varying maturities so that they come due at different times. For example, an investor might buy bonds that mature in one, three, five, and seven years, creating a "ladder" of maturities.
- **Benefits**: Laddering helps manage interest rate risk by periodically freeing up capital that can be reinvested at

higher rates if interest rates rise. It also provides regular liquidity and income, as bonds mature at different intervals.

Duration and Convexity: Assessing Bond Sensitivity to Interest Rates

- **Duration**: This is a measure of a bond's sensitivity to interest rate changes, representing the weighted average time the bondholder will receive the bond's cash flows. The longer the duration, the more sensitive the bond is to changes in interest rates.
- **Convexity**: Convexity measures the rate of change of duration as interest rates change. A bond with high convexity will be less affected by interest rate changes than a bond with low convexity, offering a sort of cushion against rate movements.
- **Application**: Understanding duration and convexity can help investors assess the risk profile of their bond investments more accurately and make more informed decisions regarding bond selection and portfolio composition.

Using Bonds for Tax-Efficient Investing

- **Tax-Exempt Bonds**: Municipal bonds are often exempt from federal income taxes and, in some cases, state and local taxes. Investing in tax-exempt bonds can be highly beneficial for investors in higher tax brackets looking to reduce their tax liability.

- **Taxable Bonds**: For investors in lower tax brackets, taxable bonds like corporate bonds or certain government securities might offer higher yields even after accounting for taxes.
- **Strategic Allocation**: By strategically allocating investments between taxable and tax-exempt bonds, investors can optimize their after-tax returns, taking into consideration their individual tax situations and market conditions.

Advanced bond investment strategies provide sophisticated investors with the tools to fine-tune their portfolios, manage risks, and enhance returns in a tax-efficient manner. Techniques such as bond laddering, understanding duration and convexity, and strategic tax planning can significantly impact the overall performance and resilience of a bond investment portfolio.

Would you like further exploration into any of these advanced strategies, insights into the bond market's current trends, or additional guidance on implementing these techniques in your investment approach?

Chapter 8

Chapter 8: Navigating the Global Bond Market

Exploring the global bond market opens a world of opportunities for investors, along with unique risks and considerations. This chapter provides an overview of the benefits and challenges of investing in foreign bonds, the impact of currency risk, and the potential of emerging market bonds.

Opportunities and Risks of Investing in Foreign Bonds

- **Diversification**: Investing in foreign bonds can significantly diversify an investment portfolio geographically, spreading risk across different economies and interest rate environments.
- **Yield Potential**: In some cases, foreign bonds may offer higher yields than domestic bonds, particularly in countries with higher interest rates.
- **Risks**: Investing in foreign bonds introduces risks such as political instability, varying levels of regulation, and economic fluctuations in the issuer's country. These factors can affect the bond's performance and the stability of returns.

How Currency Risk Affects Bond Investments

- **Currency Fluctuations**: When an investor buys foreign bonds, the investment is exposed to currency risk. If the bond's denominated currency weakens against the investor's home currency, the returns can be significantly reduced when converted back.
- **Hedging Strategies**: Currency risk can be managed through hedging strategies, such as using currency forwards or options. Some international bond funds

are hedged against currency risk, providing investors with protection against currency fluctuations.

Emerging Market Bonds

- **High Growth Potential**: Emerging market bonds can offer high yield potential due to the rapid growth and development in these markets. They can be a source of diversification and enhanced returns within a bond portfolio.
- **Volatility and Risk**: These bonds also carry higher risks, including political risk, regulatory changes, and economic volatility. The higher yield compensates for these increased risks.
- **Considerations**: Investing in emerging market bonds requires thorough research and a good understanding of the market dynamics and risks involved. Investors should consider factors such as political stability, economic policies, and the issuer's creditworthiness.

Navigating the global bond market requires an understanding of the complexities of foreign investments, including the analysis of economic indicators, political stability, and currency risks. While investing in foreign and emerging market bonds can offer attractive opportunities for diversification and yield enhancement, it also necessitates a careful assessment of the associated risks and a strategic approach to currency risk management.

Would you like to delve deeper into any specific aspect of the global bond market, such as strategies for selecting foreign bonds or more detailed methods for managing currency risk?

Chapter 9

Chapter 9: The Future of Bond Investing

As we look toward the future of bond investing, several emerging trends and innovations are shaping the landscape. This chapter explores these developments, focusing on the impact of technology and digitalization, as well as the growing importance of sustainable and green bonds.

Trends to Watch in the Bond Market

- **Increased Digitalization**: The bond market is becoming more digitized, with online platforms facilitating direct transactions, greater transparency, and improved liquidity. This trend is making bond markets more accessible to a broader range of investors.
- **Automation and AI**: Artificial intelligence and automation are playing an increasingly significant role in bond trading and portfolio management, enabling more efficient risk assessment and decision-making processes.
- **Decentralized Finance (DeFi)**: Blockchain technology and DeFi are introducing new ways to issue and trade bonds, potentially lowering costs and increasing market efficiency through tokenization of bonds and smart contracts.

The Impact of Technology and Digitalization on Bond Investing

Technology is transforming bond investing, from how investors access markets to the tools they use for analysis and trading:

- **Accessibility**: Platforms like online brokerages and apps are democratizing access to bond markets, allowing retail investors to participate more actively.
- **Data Analysis and Risk Management**: Advanced analytics and predictive models are enhancing investors' ability to assess risk and make informed decisions.
- **Operational Efficiency**: Digital platforms are streamlining the issuance, trading, and settlement of bonds, reducing costs and improving market liquidity.

Sustainable and Green Bonds

- **Sustainable Bonds**: These bonds finance projects with positive social and environmental outcomes. The market for sustainable bonds is growing rapidly as investors increasingly seek to make investments that align with their values.
- **Green Bonds**: A subset of sustainable bonds, green bonds are specifically used to fund projects that have positive environmental benefits, such as renewable energy projects, pollution control, and sustainable water management.
- **Market Growth**: The market for green and sustainable bonds is expanding, driven by investor demand,

regulatory support, and an increasing focus on climate change and sustainability issues. This growth is encouraging more issuers to consider sustainable finance options.

The future of bond investing is being shaped by technological advancements, digitalization, and a growing emphasis on sustainability. These trends are not only transforming the operational aspects of bond investing but are also redefining the types of investments that are available and desirable to both individual and institutional investors.

As we conclude this exploration of the future of bond investing, would you like to further investigate any specific trend, or is there another area of bond investing or the broader financial landscape you're interested in exploring?

Chapter 10

Chapter 10: Creating and Maintaining a Successful Bond Portfolio

In this final chapter, we consolidate our understanding of bond investments and outline strategies for longterm success. We'll cover the importance of regular portfolio reviews, staying informed about market conditions, and learning from successful bond investors. We conclude with a recap of key concepts and strategies, alongside resources for further education.

Regular Portfolio Review and Rebalancing

- **Routine Check**s: Periodically reviewing your bond portfolio is essential to ensure it aligns with your

investment goals and risk tolerance. This could mean quarterly, biannually, or annually, depending on your strategy and market volatility.
- **Rebalancing**: Over time, some investments may outper-
form others, leading to an asset allocation that doesn't fit your risk profile. Rebalancing involves selling or buying assets to return to your original allocation, ensuring that your portfolio remains well-diversified and aligned with your investment goals.

Keeping Up with Market Conditions and Economic News

- **Staying Informed**: The bond market is influenced by various factors, including economic indicators, interest rates, and monetary policy changes. Regularly following financial news and reports can help you make informed decisions and adjust your strategy as needed.
- **Adaptability**: Being adaptable and willing to adjust your investment approach in response to changing market conditions is a key to maintaining a successful bond portfolio.

Case Studies of Successful Bond Investors

Learning from the experiences and strategies of successful bond investors can provide valuable insights:

- **Diversification and Risk Management**: Many successful investors emphasize the importance of diversification across different types of bonds and

managing risk through careful selection based on credit ratings and maturities.
- **Active vs. Passive Management**: Some investors prefer a hands-off approach, focusing on bond funds or ETFs, while others actively manage their portfolios, seeking to capitalize on market inefficiencies and timing.

Conclusion: Recap of Key Concepts and Strategies

We've explored the intricacies of bond investing, from understanding bond fundamentals to building and maintaining a diversified portfolio. Key strategies include:

- Setting clear investment goals and understanding your risk tolerance.
- Diversifying across bond types, credit qualities, and maturities.
- Regular portfolio review and rebalancing to align with your investment objectives.
- Staying informed about market conditions and adjusting your strategy accordingly.

Encouragement to Continue Learning and Staying Informed

Bond investing is a dynamic field, and continuous learning is essential to navigate it successfully. Embrace new information, be open to adjusting your strategies, and stay curious about emerging trends.

Resources for Further Education

- Websites: Investopedia, Bloomberg, and Morningstar offer a wealth of information on bond investing and financial markets.
- Courses: Many online platforms like Coursera and edX provide courses on investments and finance fundamentals. • Books: "The Bond Book" by Annette Thau and "Bonds: The Unbeaten Path to Secure Investment Growth" by Hildy and
Stan Richelson are excellent reads for both beginners and experienced investors.

Appendices

- Glossary of Bond Investment Terms: A comprehensive list of terms and definitions to help you navigate the bond market.
- https://www.investopedia.com/terms/b/bond.asp

- List of Useful Websites and Online Resources: Curated list of websites for financial news, bond market analysis, and investment strategy resources.

- https://www.nerdwallet.com/article/investing/how-to-buy-bonds

- https://www.treasurydirect.gov/savings-bonds/

- https://home.treasury.gov/services/bonds-and-securities

Creating and maintaining a successful bond portfolio is a journey of continuous learning and adaptation. By staying informed, regularly reviewing your investment strategy, and learning from the experiences of successful investors, you can navigate the complexities of the bond market with confidence. Remember, the key to successful bond investing lies in understanding the fundamentals, maintaining discipline, and staying adaptable to market changes.

www.ingramcontent.com/pod-product-compliance
Lightning Source LLC
Chambersburg PA
CBHW070956220526
45471CB00007B/3053